HANDLING DATA

CONTENTS

INTRODUCTION	1
TRANSPORT TO SCHOOL	4
SCHOOL DINNERS	10
PLAYGROUND GAMES	14
TUCK SHOP	20
LITTER SURVEY	24
SPORTS RESULTS	28

About this book

This book aims to strike a balance between presenting data handling work that is grounded in relevant real-life contexts, making it purposeful and motivating for children, and providing activities designed to help children develop a grasp of key techniques and skills. The ability to understand data handling is an important real-life skill, and this is reflected in activities which focus on the interpretation of data in relevant contexts – an emphasis supported by the National Numeracy Project's definition of numeracy, which includes 'familiarity with the ways in which numerical information is gathered by counting and measuring, and is presented in graphs, charts and tables'.

In order to make the data handling relevant to the children's everyday experiences, the activities in this book take as their starting point the school and the playground. The full-colour A1 poster can be used as a starting point (see below): it illustrates all of the basic situations encountered in the activities. Within each of the book's six themes, there is opportunity – through structured whole-class discussion and involvement in group decision-making – for children to develop both their mathematical understanding of data handling and their appreciation of its real-life relevance.

A good way to reinforce this latter aspect is to find an appropriate audience for the children's findings; this might involve presenting ideas to your headteacher, school cook or caretaker, producing a newspaper report or basing an assembly on one of the themes. Mounting displays of the children's work as they proceed through these themes will motivate them further and enhance their understanding.

To complement the activities, photocopiable sheets are provided in each section which give opportunities for individual practise in basic data handling skills. As QCA have commented in a recent report on the

INTRODUCTION

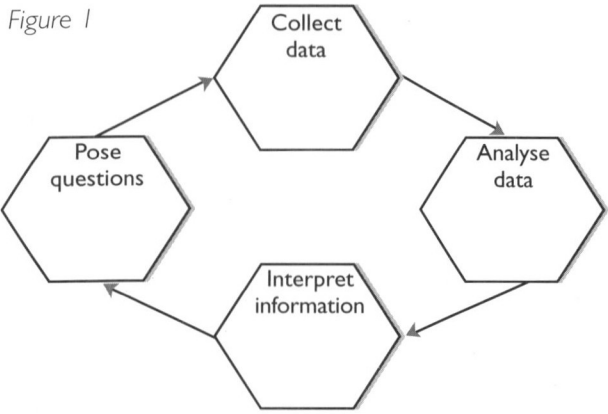

Figure 1

1997 SATs (*Standards at Year 4 – English and Mathematics*), 'Children need to have more experience of a wide range of graphs and tabulated data and to perform a variety of skills, such as reading off values, interpreting graphs, using keys given with pictograms, plotting points and completing graphs and tables'.

About data handling

It is common practice to distinguish between four aspects of data handling:

1. **Posing questions** – here, it is necessary to decide what will be investigated. In a litter survey, for example, we could look at where litter is found, when it is most prevalent or what it consists of. How we collect the data will depend on what question is posed.
2. **Collecting data** – here, we are looking for statistical evidence of some kind. This may involve designing and distributing a questionnaire, or making observations over a period of time (see the 'Playground games' section on page 14–19 for examples).
3. **Analysing data** – here, the raw data is processed to make its meaning easier to see. This may involve setting up tables, charts and/or graphs.
4. **Interpreting data** – here, conclusions are reached and related back to the original questions. Good data handling work often leads to further questions being posed.

This four-stage process is referred to as the **data handling cycle**. It is often presented diagrammatically, as in Figure 1 (which is also provided on the black and white side of the poster). It is important that time is given for developing the children's work in each of these aspects; each of the sections in this book allows for this progression. The data handling cycle diagram can also be used for planning work within each theme. Talking through the cycle regularly with the children will help them to become more aware of the whole process. Then, when the children are presented with SATs-type data handling questions (which tend to focus on interpretation only), they will have developed the skills they need to think themselves into the situation in which the questions are embedded.

Other issues

Language of data handling

It is important for the children to become confident in using the vocabulary of data handling, including the technical names of the different types of graph. An illustrated glossary of relevant terms is provided on the black and white poster (see below). Note that this glossary includes terms relevant to probability; but that probability is covered here as an aspect of data processing, rather than in relation to issues of 'chance'.

Using computers

There are great advantages to storing information on a computer database. For example, items can be added over a period of time, with different groups of children contributing; and the information can be sorted and displayed in various ways. Some types of graph, such as pie graphs and scattergrams, are much easier to produce on screen than on paper. The suggestions in this book for use of a computer database could work with any basic school database program. The 'Sports results' section includes specific guidance for setting up and interrogating a database; these principles could be applied to each of the other topic areas.

Structuring sessions

Work on each theme should begin with a whole-class discussion: looking at the poster, noting aspects of Aimhigh Primary relevant to that theme, and comparing and contrasting these with your own school. Areas for investigation should be established, and there should be regular recapping of key data handling skills.

During group or individual work – which typically might involve designing questionnaires, compiling statistical information or filling in a photocopiable sheet – it is useful to employ a number of strategies for differentiation. In some instances, this occurs where children are investigating different aspects of the same theme (for example, 'What is your favourite school dinner?' and 'How can we improve the nutritional content of school dinners?'). In other cases, the activity sheets have more probing questions for the more able children. The topics need not be followed in any particular order, and each contains activities and ideas for the full ability range. The photocopiable sheets for each section can also be used, independently of the lesson plans, for reinforcement or revision work.

INTRODUCTION

When the children are carrying out their own investigations, some general principles can be applied in order to differentiate. Older or more able children can survey a larger number of people, use more open-ended questions (such as *What is your favourite game?*) and have a free choice over which type of graph to draw. Younger or less confident children can survey a more limited sample of people using multiple-choice questions (such as *Do you prefer to play marbles, tag or hopscotch?*) and should be directed towards appropriate types of graph.

Each session should end with a plenary in which the children report on their work, or in which the key points are reinforced.

Preparing to use the poster

The A1 colour poster shows the playground and surrounding area of Aimhigh Primary School. This imaginary school is used as a backdrop for many of the activities. It would be useful to begin the work with a general discussion about the similarities and differences between this picture and your own school (see 'Let's look at the poster' below). Make sure that the poster is placed where it is visible to all. When starting any particular section of work from this book, you can use the colour poster as a starting point.

The black and white side of the poster provides three photocopiable mini-posters. The A2 glossary poster can be used for reference throughout the data handling work. The children can compare their own graphs with those displayed, and use the vocabulary when writing reports on their data handling work. The A3 data handling cycle poster can be used by the children to plan an activity and to review their efforts. The A3 sports results poster is used for the activities in that section of the book (see pages 28–32).

LET'S LOOK AT THE POSTER

GROUP SIZE AND ORGANIZATION
Whole class.
DURATION
30 minutes.
LEARNING OBJECTIVES
To formulate questions for investigation about the school and its environment. To note similarities and differences between Aimhigh Primary and the children's own school.

YOU WILL NEED
The colour poster; a flip chart and marker pens (or chalkboard and chalk).

WHAT TO DO
Display the poster for a couple of days before the session, and draw the children's attention to it. In the session, gather the children around the poster and ask them what they have noticed about it. Ask some of the following questions, noting their responses on the flip chart:
◆ *How is it like/unlike our school?*
◆ *What size are the buildings: bigger or smaller than ours?*
◆ *Is it an older building? Does it have more pupils?*
◆ *What activities are the children at Aimhigh Primary doing? How are they similar to (or different from) the playground activities that happen in this school?*

Now tell the children that they are going to do some data handling work about their school. Explain data handling simply in terms of surveys and graphs at this stage. Look at the poster again: *What questions would be interesting to investigate?*

Ask the children, working in pairs or small groups, to come up with one or two ideas that would be interesting to study. If some children are struggling to make suggestions, draw their attention to a particular part of the poster such as the litter or the kitchen. Ask the groups to share their ideas, and tell them that many of these will be followed up in their data handling work.

Follow this either by revising some important data handling vocabulary (see the glossary mini-poster) or by leading into the first section of data handling activities.

TRANSPORT TO SCHOOL

TRAVELLING TO SCHOOL

GROUP SIZE AND ORGANIZATION
Whole class, then individual work.
DURATION
45 minutes.
LEARNING OBJECTIVES
To formulate questions for investigation. To construct a bar graph from data. To interpret the data. To become familiar with the data handling cycle.

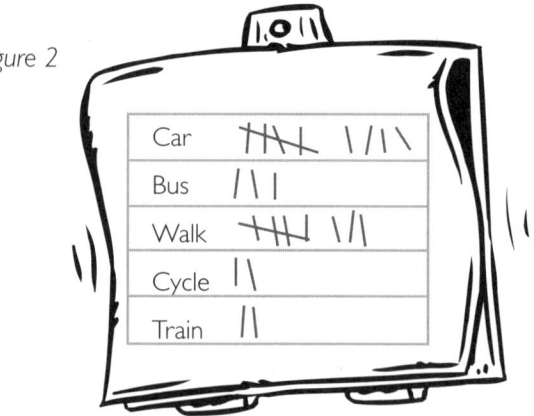

Figure 2

YOU WILL NEED
The colour poster; a map of the area around the school; an A3 copy of the data handling cycle mini-poster; the glossary mini-poster (optional); squared paper, pencils, rulers; a flip chart and marker pens (or chalkboard and chalk).

WHAT TO DO
Look at the colour poster with the class, identifying the different means of transport being used. Show the children a map of the local area; ask them where on the map they live and how they travel to school. *How can we find out which is the most common method of travelling to school?* Draw up a list of the different means of transport on the board. Remind the children of the standard method for tallying (in fives with four strokes down, then one across). Ask each child in turn to say how he or she travels to school, scribing (or having a volunteer scribe) the tally marks. Where a child uses more than one mode of transport (for example, bus and walking), he or she should indicate which mode is used for most of the distance. Write the total next to each set of tally marks, as in Figure 2.

Explain to the children that they will use this information to draw a bar graph. Remind them of the techniques needed for this: labelling the axes, giving the graph a title, using a ruler and so on. (You could use the graphs on the glossary mini-poster as examples.) It is important to note that the bars on the graph should have gaps between them, indicating that the information is **discrete**: the categories represent different things, not different amounts of the same thing.

Now the children should work individually to draw a graph. Bring them back together and ask them to tell you what the graph shows. Ask questions such as: *Which is the most common means of transport? Which is the least common? How many more children walk than travel by car?*

Show the class an A3 copy of the data handling cycle mini-poster. Talk through this diagram (also see Figure 1 on page 2). The children will return to it at other times during data handling work, and use it as a reference point. The more familiar they become with the cycle, the more effectively they will be able to make sense of the statistical information they are provided with.

Now use the cycle to discuss what the children have done:

TRANSPORT TO SCHOOL

- ◆ **Pose question:** *Which is the most common means of transport to school?*
- ◆ **Collect data:** asking everybody the question; drawing up the tally chart.
- ◆ **Analyse data:** constructing the graph.
- ◆ **Interpret data:** drawing conclusions from the graph. Good data handling activities often throw up a range of new questions. Ask the children: *Would all the classes in the school have approximately the same number of children using each method of transport? What would a bar graph showing all the children in the school look like? Would there be the same distribution in every school?*

ASSESSMENT
Note whether the children can draw an accurate graph of the information and make sensible statements about what the graph shows. Look for evidence that they are beginning to understand the data handling cycle.

IDEAS FOR DIFFERENTIATION
Older or more able children could include children from other classes in their survey. Younger children may benefit from using prepared graph axes.

TRANSPORT TO AIMHIGH PRIMARY

GROUP SIZE AND ORGANIZATION
Whole class, then groups.
DURATION
45 minutes.
LEARNING OBJECTIVE
To interpret a range of graphs and charts.
To understand the difference between discrete and continuous data.

YOU WILL NEED
Photocopiable page 8; squared paper, pencils, rulers. To prepare for this session, ask the children to find out how long their journey to school takes.

WHAT TO DO
Start by identifying with the children the two factors that determine how much time their journey to school takes: the distance and the means of transport. Explain that in this activity, they will only be concerned with the **time** taken for the journey; someone living further away, but travelling by car, might well have a shorter journey time than someone living nearby who walks. Ask the children how the data of their journey times could be recorded. Establish why it would not be sensible to draw up a tally chart for each single-minute interval.

Give each child a copy of photocopiable page 8. The bar graph on this sheet shows an example of **grouped data**. There is no need for gaps between the bars, because there is a continuum of possible times for the journey. The bars represent journeys of 0–5 minutes, 5–10 minutes, 10–15 minutes and so on. A child taking exactly 10 minutes would be placed in the 10–15 minutes category (which is technically 10–14.99 minutes). This data can be contrasted with the **discrete** data in the previous activity. Read through the questions with the class; then ask them to work individually to answer the questions. They should use the graph in Part A as a model for their own graph in Part B, drawing on a sheet of squared paper.

ASSESSMENT
In part A of the photocopiable sheet, can the children interpret the information correctly? The answers are: **1.** 20–25 minutes. **2.** 10–15 minutes. **3.** More than 15 minutes. **4.** Less than 20 minutes. In part B, can the children construct a tally chart and a bar graph from the raw data?

IDEAS FOR DIFFERENTIATION
More able children could draw up a plan for collecting data from the whole school about their journeys to school; some might begin to compile a computer database on this theme.

TRANSPORT TO SCHOOL

SCHOOL ON THE MOVE

GROUP SIZE AND ORGANIZATION
Whole class, then smaller groups.
DURATION
45 minutes.
LEARNING OBJECTIVE
To construct graphs using a scaling factor.

YOU WILL NEED
Centimetre squared paper; other types of graph paper; pencils, rulers. Information from the whole school about their journey times and means of transport when coming to school will need to have been collected beforehand, perhaps as an extension activity during the previous two sessions. Alternatively, copy and use the data for Aimhigh Primary given in Figure 3. If your school is quite small (fewer than 100 pupils), it will be preferable to use the Aimhigh data. At the start of the session, the information should be available to the children – either in photocopied form or written on the flip chart.

WHAT TO DO
Remind the children of the graphs they have drawn for whole-class information about means of transport and journey time. Now ask them to consider the whole-school data: *What would happen if we tried to plot this information on this centimetre squared paper?* We would need a very large sheet of paper. To solve this problem, introduce the idea of a **scaling factor**. Ask the children to count up the squares on an A4 sheet of centimetre squared paper and consider whether a scale of 1cm for two children will fit. *If not, what would be a sensible scale to use: 1cm for 4 children? For 5 children?* Encourage them to experiment with different scale factors and types of graph paper.

ASSESSMENT
Note whether the children can draw accurate graphs from the data. Do they understand the concept of a scale factor?

IDEAS FOR DIFFERENTIATION
Older or more able children could experiment with further scale factors and more types of graph paper. Less confident children may need support to choose a scale and mark the axes; they could use a calculator to help them work out the number of squares needed.

Figure 3

Aimhigh Primary (260 pupils)
Means of transport to school

Car	105
Bus	28
Walk	82
Cycle	30
Train	15

TRANSPORT TO SCHOOL

TRUE OR FALSE?

GROUP SIZE AND ORGANIZATION
Pairs within groups of 4 or 6; whole class for review.
DURATION
45 minutes.
LEARNING OBJECTIVES
To interpret a range of graphs and charts.
To use mathematical reasoning.

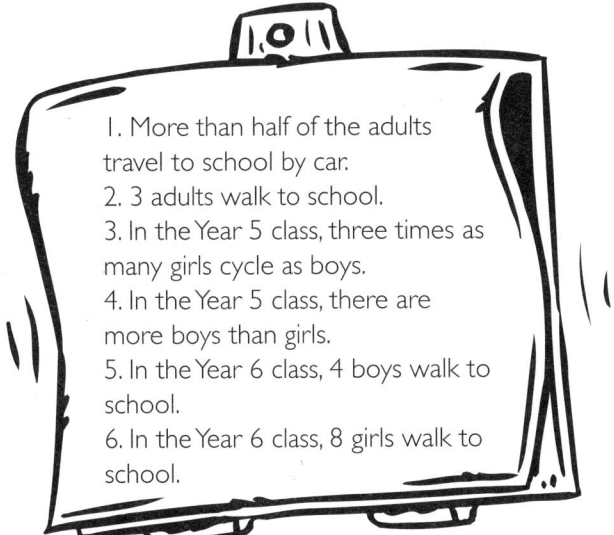

1. More than half of the adults travel to school by car.
2. 3 adults walk to school.
3. In the Year 5 class, three times as many girls cycle as boys.
4. In the Year 5 class, there are more boys than girls.
5. In the Year 6 class, 4 boys walk to school.
6. In the Year 6 class, 8 girls walk to school.

Figure 4

YOU WILL NEED
Photocopiable page 9; a flip chart or board displaying the questions shown in Figure 4.

WHAT TO DO
NB The types of graph shown on photocopiable page 9 are the same as those in the corresponding activity in the 'School dinners' section (see page 10); the latter sheet is intended to provide further practice in interpreting data, and can be used even if the whole topic is not being studied. Alternatively, one sheet could be used in class and the other for homework.

This activity complements the children's investigations using real-life data by providing opportunities to interpret a set of pre-drawn graphs and charts. You may prefer to have the whole class working on this activity simultaneously. Alternatively, some children could do this activity while others conduct a survey for another activity; the groups could then swap tasks. This would overcome the difficulty of the whole class trying to carry out a survey at the same time.

Give a copy of photocopiable page 9 to each child or pair (enlarge to A3 size if shared). Read through the headings together, checking that everyone understands the information shown in each figure. Working in pairs, the children should consider the statements on the flip chart and decide whether each is true or false. They should make a note of their reasons, then check with other pairs in their groups. When each group is agreed about each statement, each pair should write two more statements (either true or false) related to the information shown in each of the three diagrams (making six statements in all). They can try these with other pairs or the whole class later, during a review of the work.

ASSESSMENT
Note whether the children can interpret information from a range of graphs and charts in order to evaluate the statements, as follows: 1. True, 2. False, 3. False, 4. True, 5. True, 6. False. Can they justify their answers?

IDEAS FOR DIFFERENTIATION
With younger or less confident children, cut up the copies of page 9 and ask them to consider only one or two of the figures (the Carroll and Venn diagrams are simpler than the pie chart) with the corresponding statements. More able children could make up further statements for each figure.

FURTHER RESEARCH
Older or more able children could undertake further research on this theme to answer questions such as:
◆ *What is the average journey time from home to school of the children in the class/school?*
◆ *Does travelling home take longer than travelling to school?*
◆ *Does the whole class spend more or less than 24 hours travelling to school and back home each day?*
◆ *Find out how many bus, car and train journeys different families make each day.*

HANDLING DATA

TRANSPORT TO SCHOOL

Name _____ Date _____

The journey to school: times

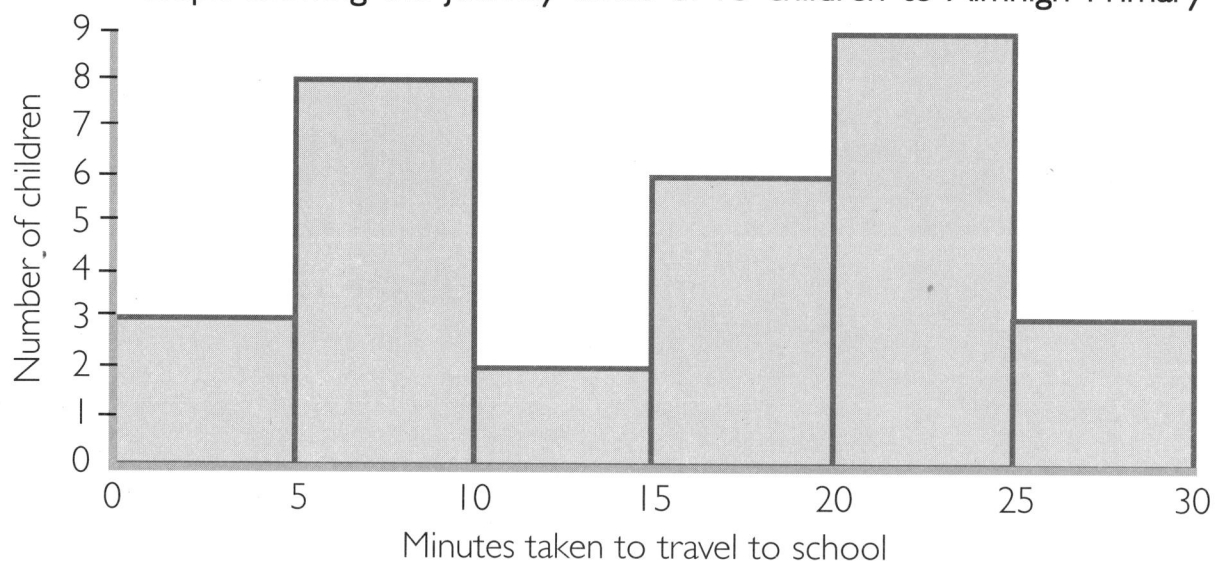

Graph showing the journey times of Y3 children to Aimhigh Primary

A. Look at this graph and answer the questions below.
1. Which is the most common journey time? _____
2. Which is the least common journey time? _____
3. Do more children take more than 15 minutes or less than 15 minutes? _____
4. Do more children take more than 20 minutes or less than 20 minutes? _____

B. The table below shows the journey times for the Year 4 children at Aimhigh Primary. Use it to complete the tally chart. Then draw a bar graph to show this information.

Time in minutes	Tally	No. of children
0–5		
5–10		
10–15		
15–20		
20–25		
25–30		

Times in minutes taken by the children in Y4 to travel to school							
6	7½	11	19½	8¼	6	14	23
25	4	8	12	13	27	19	15½
17	21	3½	19¼	16	26	24	17
4	6	11	14	17	13	22	20½

TRANSPORT TO SCHOOL

Name _____ Date _____

The journey to school: means of transport

One group in Year 5 drew this pie chart to show how the 20 adults working at Aimhigh Primary travelled to the school:

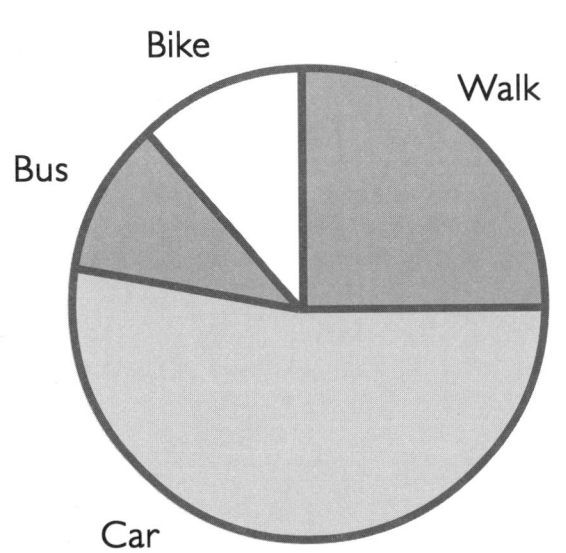

A group of Year 5 children drew this Carroll diagram to show how the boys and girls in their class travelled to school:

	CAR	BUS	BIKE	WALK
BOYS	4	5	2	5
GIRLS	4	2	5	4

In Year 6 there are 30 children. After collecting information from the whole class, one group drew this Venn diagram:

GIRLS   CHILDREN WALKING TO SCHOOL

8 7 4

SCHOOL DINNERS

SCHOOL DINNER SURVEYS

GROUP SIZE AND ORGANIZATION
Whole class, then groups.
DURATION
Two 50-minute sessions.
LEARNING OBJECTIVES
To formulate problems for investigation. To practise constructing bar graphs. To interpret data. To be aware of the data handling cycle.

YOU WILL NEED
The colour poster; squared paper, pencils, rulers; the glossary and data handling cycle mini-posters; a flip chart and marker pens (or chalkboard and chalk). The co-operation of the school kitchen staff, and of another class teacher, will be needed.

WHAT TO DO
Look at the poster with the class; point out that even early in the morning, people are already working in the kitchen. Discuss the work involved in preparing school dinners – you might invite the school cook to talk to your class, or arrange for them to have a supervised visit to the kitchen. Ask the children to suggest ideas for school dinner investigations, such as:
◆ *How many children stay for school dinners, bring sandwiches or go home for lunch?*
◆ *What is our favourite meal?*
◆ *What would we like to see on the menu?*
Such questions could obviously prove to be sensitive; it is important to guide the children towards making positive suggestions rather than being over-critical. In order to give them a sense of purpose, it would be a good idea to arrange for them to present their findings and suggestions to the headteacher or cook. Ask each group to focus on one question and to discuss what information they need to find out in order to answer it: what they need to ask, how they will record the answers, and who in their group will do what. It is important that they think about the practicalities of data collection before rushing off to do it. Make sure that the groups are investigating different questions.

Now let the children survey their classmates or visit another class to collect information. They could do this a group at a time while other work is going on, or during break or lunchtime. By the start of the second session, the children should have finished collecting data. They should reflect on the questions they have asked and think about what kinds of graph they could draw; look at the examples on the glossary mini-poster with the class. Each child should draw a graph from his or her group's data, paying attention to scale, labelling of axes and so on.

Bring the children back together and ask each group to tell you what they have found out. Write their findings on the flip chart. Now show the class the data handling cycle mini-poster (or an A3 copy of it) and talk through it in relation to the children's work. What further questions might they now want to ask?

The children can work individually or in groups to write up a report of the class's findings, using some of their tables and graphs to illustrate it. They can use the four headings of the data handling cycle to structure their writing. The reports can be displayed or passed on to the headteacher or head cook.

ASSESSMENT
Can the children formulate sensible questions for investigation; collect the data; draw an accurate graph; and make sensible statements about what the graph shows? Are they beginning to understand the data handling cycle?

DIFFERENTIATION
Older or more able children could undertake more extensive surveying of other classes, or use a questionnaire with several questions rather than a single one. They could also use a computer database to compile the data.

DINNER CHOICES

GROUP SIZE AND ORGANIZATION
Individual or small-group work.
DURATION
40 minutes.
LEARNING OBJECTIVES
To collect and analyse data. To investigate combinations.

YOU WILL NEED
Photocopiable page 12, pencils.

WHAT TO DO
Give the children a copy each of photocopiable page 12. Ask them to imagine that they are pupils at Aimhigh Primary, where the new chef has devised a special three-course menu for Fridays only. The children should make their own choices (one selection for each of the three courses) and then survey their

SCHOOL DINNERS

friends' choices before answering the questions. There is space on the sheet for information from nine children (in abbreviated form); you could suggest that a minimum of six responses (their own plus five others) is needed to answer the questions.

For question 3, the children will need a systematic way to record the different possible combinations; you may need to discuss this with them. There are 24 possible combinations (two choices of starter × four choices of main course × three choices of dessert). For most classes, it will therefore be impossible for all the children to choose a unique meal.

ASSESSMENT
Do the children work systematically to find different combinations of the dinner options?

IDEAS FOR DIFFERENTIATION
More able children could try to find all the possible combinations if the menu offers three different starters. For less able children, having fewer choices of main course and dessert will make the task easier.

TRUE OR FALSE?

GROUP SIZE AND ORGANIZATION
Pairs within groups of 4 or 6; whole class for review.
DURATION
45 minutes.
LEARNING OBJECTIVES
To interpret a range of graphs and charts. To use mathematical reasoning.

YOU WILL NEED
Photocopiable page 13, pencils; a flip chart or board displaying the statements shown in Figure 5.

> In the Year 6 class, the majority have a school dinner.
> In the Year 6 class, fewer than 15 children have a school dinner.
> In the Year 3 class, twice as many boys as girls choose jelly.
> In the Year 3 class, more girls like ice cream than fruit salad and jelly altogether.
> In the Year 4 class, 10 boys have a school dinner.
> In the Year 4 class, 6 children's favourite meal is fish fingers.

Figure 5

WHAT TO DO
Give each child or pair a copy of photocopiable page 13 (enlarged to A3 size if shared). The graph types are the same as those in the corresponding activity in the 'Transport' section (see page 13), where the organization of this activity is described in detail.

ASSESSMENT
See page 10. The answers are: 1. True, 2. False, 3. False, 4. False, 5. True, 6. False.

IDEAS FOR DIFFERENTIATION
See page 10.

EXTENSION WORK
Ask the school cook for information about the quantities of different items used each week: vegetables, eggs, fruits, packets of ingredients and so on. The figures only need to be approximate. Discuss with the children how they might set up a bar graph to show the amounts of different items used. It may be necessary to round the numbers to the nearest ten or hundred. Let some of the children create the graph on a computer to show how the computer can resize a graph automatically to fit onto a page. (The computer is also useful for handling 'awkward' data: it does not require larger numbers to be rounded, and can find a suitable scale automatically.) With older or more able children, you could use weights (in kilograms) rather than packets for items such as sugar, salt and flour.

FURTHER RESEARCH
Older or more able children could carry out further research on this theme to answer questions such as:
◆ *How efficient is the queuing system in the dining hall? How might it be improved?*
◆ *How much food is wasted each week?*
◆ *What is the nutritional content of the different meals?*

SCHOOL DINNERS

Name _____ Date _____

Aimhigh Primary – menu for Friday

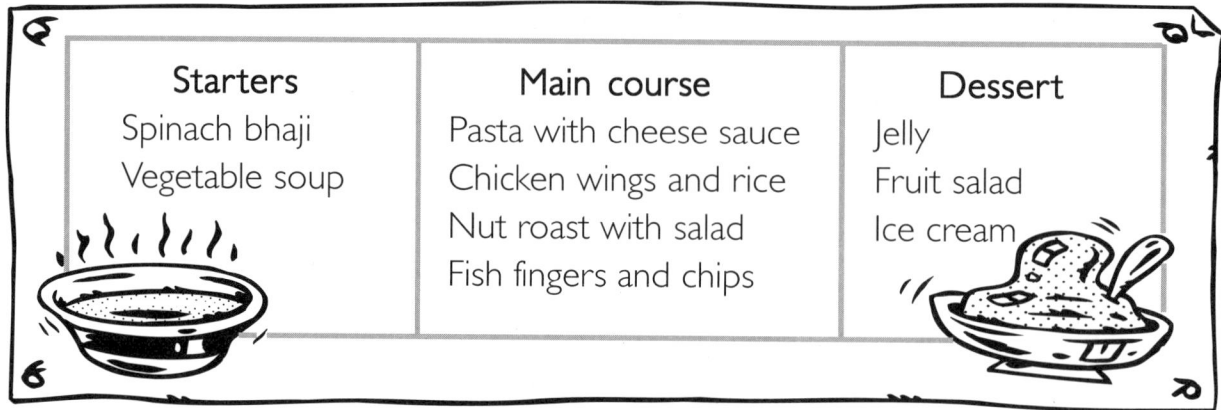

Starters	Main course	Dessert
Spinach bhaji	Pasta with cheese sauce	Jelly
Vegetable soup	Chicken wings and rice	Fruit salad
	Nut roast with salad	Ice cream
	Fish fingers and chips	

◆ What would you choose? Complete the choices for yourself and some friends.

Name: _____	Name: _____	Name: _____
Starter: _____	Starter: _____	Starter: _____
Main: _____	Main: _____	Main: _____
Dessert: _____	Dessert: _____	Dessert: _____
Name: _____	Name: _____	Name: _____
Starter: _____	Starter: _____	Starter: _____
Main: _____	Main: _____	Main: _____
Dessert: _____	Dessert: _____	Dessert: _____
Name: _____	Name: _____	Name: _____
Starter: _____	Starter: _____	Starter: _____
Main: _____	Main: _____	Main: _____
Dessert: _____	Dessert: _____	Dessert: _____

1. For your group, which is:
 - the most popular starter? _____ the least popular? _____
 - the most popular main course? _____ the least popular? _____
 - the most popular dessert? _____ the least popular? _____

2. Did you and your friends all choose different combinations of the courses?

3. Would it be possible for everyone in your class to have a different combination?

SCHOOL DINNERS

Name _____   Date _____

Dinner data

One group in Year 6 drew a pie chart to show what kind of meal the 30 children in the class ate at lunchtime:

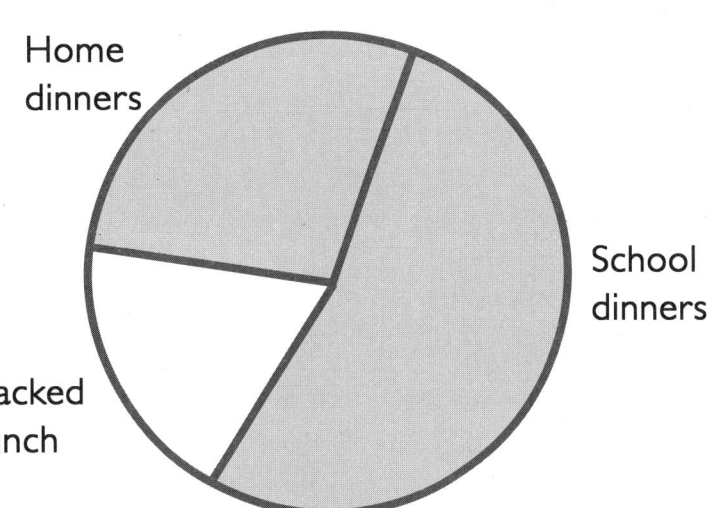

A group of Year 3 children drew this Carroll diagram to show their class's favourite desserts:

	JELLY	ICE CREAM	FRUIT SALAD
BOYS	5	3	9
GIRLS	3	7	4

A group of Year 4 children drew this Venn diagram, based on the 19 children in their class who had school dinners:

BOYS   FAVOURITE MEAL: FISH FINGERS

HANDLING DATA   RESOURCE BANK   13

PLAYGROUND GAMES

IN THE PLAYGROUND

GROUP SIZE AND ORGANIZATION
Whole class, then groups.
DURATION
Two 1-hour sessions.
LEARNING OBJECTIVES
To identify questions for investigation. To analyse and interpret data.

YOU WILL NEED
The poster (both sides); a flip chart and marker pens (or chalkboard and chalk); blank A3 paper, squared paper, pencils.

WHAT TO DO
Look at the colour poster with the class. Ask the children to identify the different games and sports that are being played. List these on the flip chart. Ask the children to think about how their own playground is used: *Do you play the same games as these? What are your favourite games? Which children use which parts of the playground? Do you have a favourite place? Do boys and girls use the same areas? Do older and younger children use the same areas? What games are played at different times of the year?*

Now ask the children to draw a rough plan of the playground, indicating what the different areas are used for. Suggest that they use symbols for the different activities (for example, a skipping rope, a marble and so on) and draw matchstick figures (different sizes for older and younger children, different colours for girls and boys). If possible, have this discussion before break; the children can then look around at break-time and draw up their plans on returning to the classroom.

At the same time as they are working on their plans, they should try to think of a suitable question for data collection about playground use. Drawing the plans will help to stimulate ideas – for example:
◆ *What is the favourite game of the infants/juniors?*
◆ *Do boys and girls have equal use of space?*
◆ *Do boys and girls play together?*
◆ *Do younger and older children play together?*
◆ *Are the same games played before school, in morning break, at lunchtime and in afternoon break?*
◆ *What do the teachers and assistants think about the children's use of the playground?*
◆ *How could the playground be improved?*

You may choose to direct particular groups to particular questions; and there may be issues that the children wish to investigate. As well as completing their playground plans, the children should form small groups to identify a question they would like to work on. They should discuss what they will need to do to find an answer; this might involve observing other children during playtimes, questioning different groups of children, or talking with teachers and other playtime supervisors. They should make a proposal stating how they intend to do this.

The session can end with a whole-class discussion of the children's ideas. You should vet their ideas for practicality before they begin their surveys. See the note on differentiation in the Introduction (page 2) for further guidance about children's questions.

NB Some possible questions on this topic raise equal opportunity issues in relation to boys' and girls' use of playground space or younger children's access to certain areas. Many schools have a policy with regard to playground behaviour; but a policy on the use of different areas is less common. It may be that the children's work on this topic will lead to their making proposals for appropriate rules. Presenting results from surveys and questionnaires is a good way to support any such proposals, and will give the children a sense of purpose in their data handling work.

PLAYGROUND GAMES

Before the second session, the children need to have the opportunity to collect their data. Allow a week's interval for this, since it may involve children spending several playtimes observing other children, talking to adults or giving children in other classes questionnaires to complete. An alternative, if time is limited, would be to conduct the survey within your own class only. This loses the wider perspective; but perhaps a colleague could carry out a similar pair of lessons with his or her class, and the children could be encouraged to compare and contrast the two sets of results.

After a few minutes to recap the questions and the purposes of the data collecting, the children should spend most of the second session drawing graphs and charts to represent their findings. They should be reminded to keep in mind the question(s) they had set out to ask, and use the data to find evidence relevant to it. You should also offer the usual reminders about giving each graph a title and labelling the axes.

For the second half of the session, bring the children back together and ask each group to tell you what they have found out. They can refer to the glossary mini-poster for appropriate vocabulary. Write up their findings on the flip chart. Now show the class the data handling cycle mini-poster and talk through it in relation to this topic. Ask the children to say what their original question was, how the data was collected and analysed, and what conclusions they can draw.

Working in groups or individually, the children can write up a report of the class's findings. They should use some of their tables and graphs to illustrate what they have found, and be aware of the data handling cycle (they could use its four headings to structure their writing). Their reports can be displayed or passed to the headteacher.

ASSESSMENT
In the first session, can the children make reasonable observations about playground activities? Can they formulate sensible questions and propose a practical way to collect the data? In the second session, can they use the data they have collected to draw an accurate graph? Can they make sensible statements about what their graph shows? Are they beginning to understand the data handling cycle?

DIFFERENTIATION
The children could work in mixed-ability groups for this activity. With some groups, you may prefer to suggest the best format for their graphs. More confident children could record their data onto a computer database.

AROUND THE SNAKE

GROUP SIZE AND ORGANIZATION
Whole class.
DURATION
1 hour.
LEARNING OBJECTIVE
To consider the fairness of a game, based on a number of trials.

YOU WILL NEED
The colour poster; the glossary mini-poster; photocopiable page 18 (this can be copied onto card and laminated for repeated use); one 1–6 dice per pair; a flipchart and marker pen (or chalkboard and chalk); paper, pencils.

WHAT TO DO
Spend a few minutes revising some of the language of probability, as it is used in relation to data handling (see the glossary mini-poster). Next, look at the poster with the class and point out the hopscotch grid. Ask the children to suggest other playground games which involve grids or markings. Give out copies of photocopiable page 18 (one between two) and read through the rules. (If you can draw this grid in your playground, the game can be introduced as a 'people game' with two children playing the parts of the counters.)

Ask the children to discuss whether or not the game is a **fair** one. Establish that in a fair game, both

PLAYGROUND GAMES

players have an **even chance** of winning. After hearing their opinions, ask them to predict who will win more often if the game is played 10 times: the person throwing the dice or the person moving 3 spaces each time. Each pair can now play the game, taking it in turns to go first and keeping a tally of the results.

After all the pairs have played the game 10 times, the class should stop. Ask each pair to call out their results; add up the 'Wins for the 3' and the 'Wins for the dice thrower' on the flip chart. With 15 pairs of children each playing the game 10 times, there ought to be a clear majority of wins for the dice throwers. If a child asks why this is, explain that the **mean score** on the dice is (1 + 2 + 3 + 4 + 5 + 6) ÷ 6 = 3.5. Discuss why, in order to judge the fairness of this kind of game, it is important to play the game many times over.

Ask the children how the game could be made fairer. The usual suggestion is to pitch the dice thrower against a steady move of 4, but this will actually weight the odds against the dice thrower. The children could try this out; some pairs could also play with a dice thrower against a steady move of 2 or 5, which will make the unfairness of the game more obvious.

Encourage the children to write an account of their work, discussing the game, their predictions and what they have found out.

ASSESSMENT
Can the children make reasoned comments about the fairness of the game? Can they use tally marks to keep track of their results?

DIFFERENTIATION
More able children could experiment with snakes of different lengths. Does making the snake shorter or longer affect the likelihood of either player winning against a constant move of 3? (The longer the snake, the better the dice-thrower's chance of winning, since the luck of individual throws will balance out.)

OVER THE WALL

GROUP SIZE AND ORGANIZATION
Whole class.
DURATION
1 hour.
LEARNING OBJECTIVE
To consider strategies for increasing the chances of winning a game, based on the results of a probability experiment.

YOU WILL NEED
The colour poster; photocopiable page 19 (this can be copied onto card and laminated for repeated use); two 1–6 dice per pair; 30 counters or small cubes per pair; squared paper, blank paper, pencils; a flip chart and marker pen (or chalkboard and chalk).

WHAT TO DO
Start in the hall (the end of a PE lesson is ideal for this). Divide the class into two equal-sized groups, one either side of a bench representing the 'wall'. Each child should choose a number between 2 and 12 and write it on a piece of paper. One child in each team is nominated as a dice thrower; these children should take it in turns to throw two dice and add up the score. If the total corresponds to a number held by any child in the same team, that child can 'jump the wall' to the other side and is out of the game. If more than one child has the number thrown, then only one child can move; the others with that number must wait until it comes up again.

Although you can play until the last child from one of the teams jumps the wall, it is less frustrating to declare the team with the most members across the wall after five minutes as the winners. After playing a couple of times, ask the children: *What might be a good strategy for winning the game?* The usual response will be for the team to have a good selection of numbers between them; but is that necessarily the best strategy?

Back in the classroom, look at the colour poster with the class. Point out the children playing the 'Over the wall' game. Ask the children to test possible strategies by playing the game in pairs. Give each pair a copy of photocopiable page 19, two dice and 30 counters. Remind them of the rules. Let them play the game two or three times; then discuss strategies with the class. Some children may have noticed that scores of 5 to 9 come up more frequently than the others,

PLAYGROUND GAMES

and some may have decided not to put any counters on 2 or 12 (which come up least frequently). A good way to illustrate this pattern is to ask each pair to throw the two dice 100 times, keeping a tally of the answers. They can then plot the results as a bar graph and note the pattern of totals that emerges. They should see that there is a humped or **'normal distribution'** which peaks at the central numbers 6, 7 and 8. The pattern will be even clearer if several pairs combine their results.

A good way to explain this pattern is to draw up a combination table on the flip chart and ask children to complete it by writing in the total for each combination of dice (see Figure 6). It will then be clear that in every 36 throws, there is only one chance of getting a total of 2 or of 12, whereas 7 occurs six times and 8 and 6 five times each. Of course, this indicates only the theoretical likelihood; the distribution curve which emerges when the results of 100 throws are graphed is the experimental evidence, which may differ slightly from the theoretical outcome. Explain that the greater the amount of evidence obtained, the closer the actual results should be to the theoretical outcome.

The children can now discuss further what would be the best strategy. Should they put all their counters on 6, 7 and 8? Should they still distribute them more widely along the grid? Is it worth putting any counters on the 2 or the 12? What about the 3 or the 11?

Conclude the work on this topic with a final whole-class game. Note whether the teams have changed their tactics in the light of experience.

ASSESSMENT

Can the children formulate a strategy for the game? Can they explain their results by referring to probability?

FURTHER RESEARCH

Older or more able children could research this theme further. For example, they could:
◆ find out what games their parents and grandparents played when at school;
◆ use penpals or e-mail contacts to find out about playground games around the world (reference books might also help with this);
◆ use any number grids in the school playground as the basis for a game – or design a grid and invent a game to play on it.

Figure 6

First dice score

+	1	2	3	4	5	6
1						
2						
3						
4						
5						
6						

Second dice score

PLAYGROUND GAMES

Name _____ Date _____

Around the snake

A game for two players with a counter each and one 1–6 dice.

Rules

1. Both players start with their counters on the head of the snake.
2. Take it in turns to move. One player moves forward 3 spaces each turn; the other player throws the dice and moves the number that comes up.
3. The first player to reach the end of the snake wins.

◆ Is this a fair game? Is it better to throw the dice or to move 3 spaces each time?

PLAYGROUND GAMES

Name _____   Date _____

Over the wall

A game for two players with 15 counters each and two 1–6 dice.

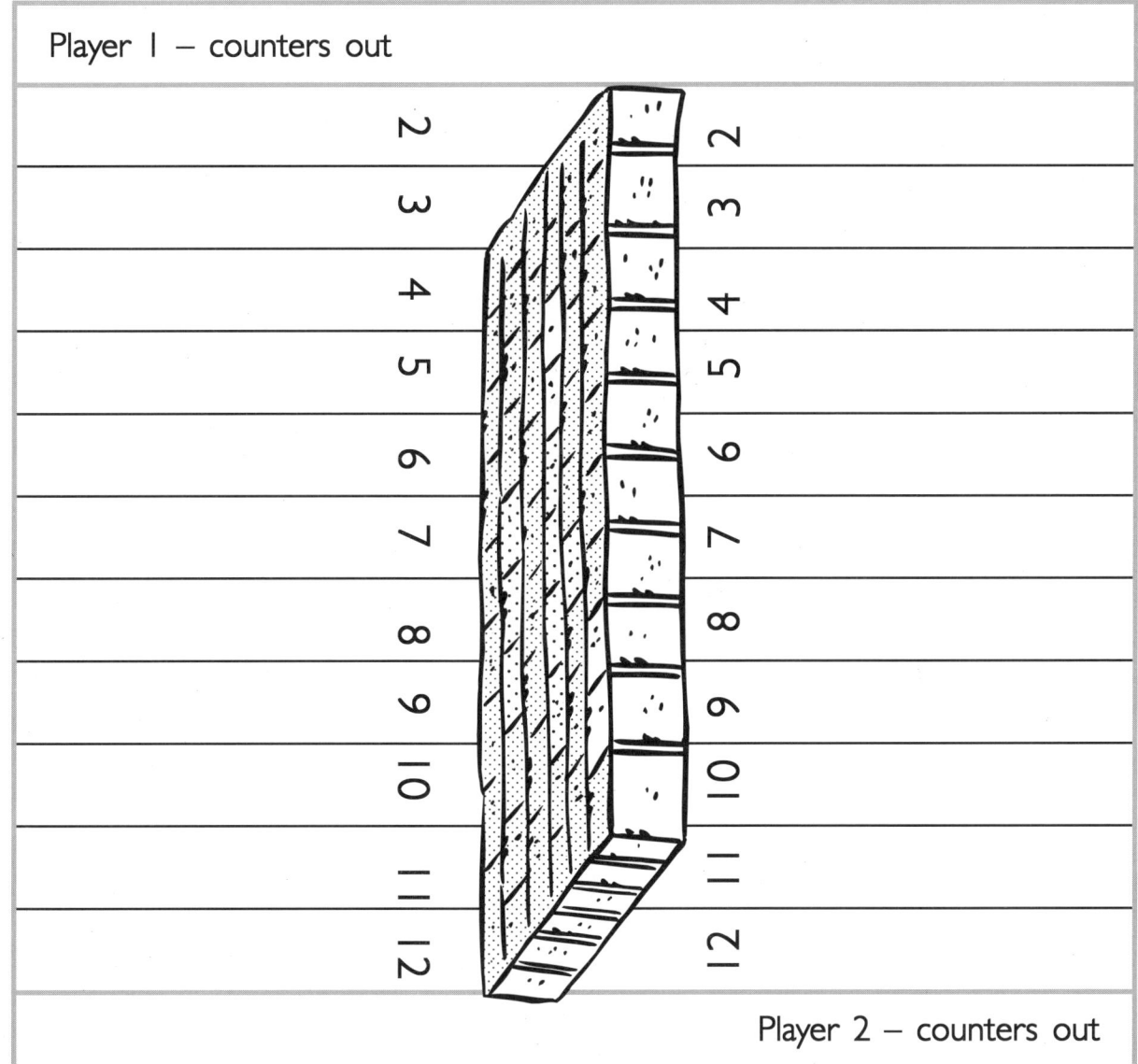

Player 1 – counters out

Player 2 – counters out

Rules

1. The players sit on either side of the wall. Each player places 15 counters on the numbers on his or her side of the wall – as many (or as few) on each number as he or she likes.
2. Take turns to throw the two dice and add up the total score. If one of your numbers comes up, you can move that counter over the wall and out of the game.
3. Play for 5 minutes, then count up how many counters you still have. The player with the fewest counters remaining is the winner.

TUCK SHOP

'TUCK-U-LIKE'

GROUP SIZE AND ORGANIZATION
Whole class, then pairs or small groups.
DURATION
One hour.
LEARNING OBJECTIVES
To formulate a question for data collection.
To collect, analyse and interpret data.

YOU WILL NEED
The colour poster; the data handling cycle mini-poster; a flip chart and marker pens (or chalkboard and chalk); paper, pencils.

WHAT TO DO
Look at the colour poster with the class, focusing on the tuck shop. *What things are on sale?* If your school has a tuck shop, ask what items it sells the greatest quantities of. If you do not have a school tuck shop, ask the children what they would like one to sell. *What things are suitable for selling? What things would be too expensive, unhealthy or a litter risk?*

On the flip chart, write a number of different questions on this theme that the children could investigate. The aim is to take the children quite quickly through the data handling cycle; straightforward questions based on children voting for their favourite items will work best. Tell the children that this survey might form the basis of a proposal to set up a school tuck shop (if you already have a school tuck shop, the survey could be used to amend the stock of items kept). The questions might include:
◆ *What is your favourite snack?*
◆ *What is your favourite crisp flavour?*
◆ *What is your favourite drink/fruit?*
◆ *How many bags of crisps do you eat in a week?* (Estimate.)
◆ *What is a sensible maximum amount of money to bring to school?*
◆ *What things would it not be good to have in the tuck shop?*

Each pair or small group should have a different question to work on. They should now conduct a quick survey of the class, making tally charts of the children's replies. Next, they should use the information to construct a bar graph or a pictogram of their findings. Finally, they should write a short paragraph stating what their graph shows.

Write up the groups' findings on the flip chart and discuss them with the whole class. Conclude by looking at the data handling cycle mini-poster and reviewing how each aspect has been fulfilled – for example:
◆ **Pose question:** *What is the most popular crisp flavour?*
◆ **Collect data:** making a tally chart of classmates' answers.
◆ **Analyse data:** drawing a pictogram or bar chart of the data.
◆ **Interpret data:** making statements based on the graph about what were the most popular and least popular flavours.

ASSESSMENT
Can the children formulate a question for data collection? Can they collect, analyse and interpret their data efficiently?

Y3 AT THE TUCK SHOP

GROUP SIZE AND ORGANIZATION
Individuals or pairs.
DURATION
50 minutes.
LEARNING OBJECTIVES
To analyse and interpret information. To construct a pictogram. To calculate with money.

YOU WILL NEED
Photocopiable page 22; pencils, coloured pencils, rough paper.

WHAT TO DO
NB This task is suitable for children in Years 3 and 4, or as revision for older children.

TUCK SHOP

Tell the class that in today's session, they will be looking at what the Year 3 class at Aimhigh Primary bought from the tuck shop in two days. Give each child a copy of photocopiable page 22 and read through it together, checking that the children have understood the questions. Give out paper for rough work. Let the children work individually or in pairs for about 30 minutes; then go through the answers with the class.

ASSESSMENT
Can the children interpret the information in the pictogram to answer the questions and fill in the table? Can they construct a similar pictogram from the information provided in question 7? The answers to the questions on page 22 are: **1.** Apples. **2.** Bananas. **3.** 4 more. **4.** 6 more. **5.** 28 items. **6.** Chews – 6, 36p; Bananas – 2, 20p; Glow lollies – 3, 27p; Crunch bars – 5, 60p; Apples – 9, 99p; Orange juice – 3, 45p. Total spent by the class: £2.87.

IDEAS FOR DIFFERENTIATION
When the children are working individually, give support to any children who are in difficulty.
Older or more able children could try to draw up a sales table for Tuesday and use it to calculate whether more money was spent on Monday or on Tuesday. They could also invent some figures for the whole week's sales and then draw a pictogram in which there is a scaling factor (for example, one food symbol to represent 5 items of that food).

SALES FIGURES

GROUP SIZE AND ORGANIZATION
Individuals or pairs.
DURATION
50 minutes.
LEARNING OBJECTIVES
To interpret a line graph. To construct a line graph. To calculate with money.

YOU WILL NEED
Photocopiable page 23; rough paper, pencils, coloured pencils; calculators.

WHAT TO DO
NB This task is suitable for children in Years 5 and 6, or for more able Year 4 children.
Tell the children that in today's session, they will be looking at the weekly sales figures from the tuck shop at Aimhigh Primary. Give each child a copy of photocopiable page 23 and read through it together, checking that the children have understood all the questions. Explain that the sales figures used in the line graph have been rounded up or down to the nearest £1. Provide calculators and rough paper for working out answers. Let the children work individually or in pairs for about 30 minutes; then go through the answers with the whole class.

ASSESSMENT
Can the children interpret the information on the line graph? Can they plot a line graph from the information given at the bottom of the sheet? The answers to the questions on the sheet are: **1.** Week 7. **2.** Week 6. **3.** Weeks 2 and 5. **4.** Weeks 4 and 5. **5.** Weeks 3 and 4. **6.** £1040. **7.** £130. **8.** Weeks 2, 3, 5 and 6. **9.** Weeks 1, 4, 7 and 8.

IDEAS FOR DIFFERENTIATION
When the children are working individually, give support to any children who are in difficulty.
Older or more able children could attempt the following problems:
◆ *Aimhigh Primary decides to donate 20% of the tuck shop's takings each week to a charity. Calculate how much the charity will receive each week.* (The percentage can be changed to make this task more or less difficult.)
◆ *Use current conversion rates to calculate the tuck shop's takings each week in francs, marks, US dollars or Euros.*

FURTHER RESEARCH
Older or more able children could research this theme further. For example, they could:
◆ use their work from the 'Tuck-U-like' activity to write a proposal for setting up and running a school tuck shop (this will need to be backed up with more facts and figures regarding potential sales);
◆ investigate the idea of setting up a class 'bring and buy' stall. What sort of items could be sold? What should the children bring? What would be sensible prices to charge?

Tuck shop pictograms

Pictogram showing the items bought by the Year 3 class in the tuck shop one Monday

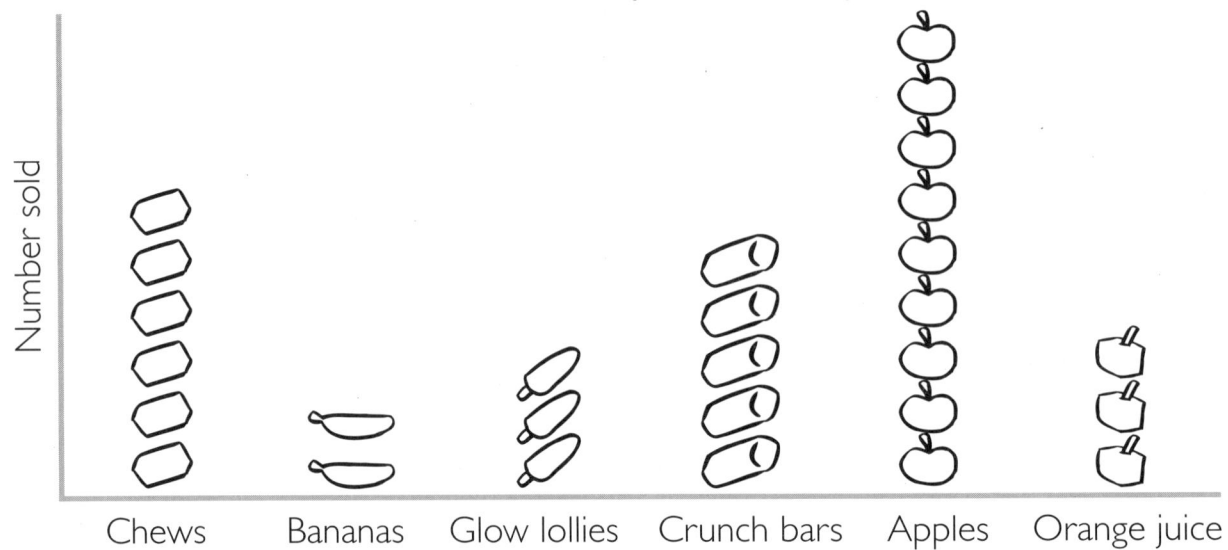

◆ Look at the graph and answer these questions:
1. Which item was the most popular? _____
2. Which item was the least popular? _____
3. How many more chews than bananas were sold? _____
4. How many more apples than glow lollies were sold? _____
5. What was the total number of items sold? _____
6. From the graph, complete the table below. Add up the figures in the final column to find out how much money was spent by the whole class.

Item	Cost for one	Number sold	Total for each item
Chews	6p		
Bananas	10p		
Glow lollies	9p		
Crunch bars	12p		
Apples	11p		
Orange juice	15p		

Total for class: _____

7. The Year 3 class bought these items on Tuesday: 3 chews, 5 bananas, 6 glow lollies, 10 crunch bars, 2 apples, 3 orange juice cartons. Draw a pictogram to show this information.

TUCK SHOP

Name _____ Date _____

Tuck shop line graphs
Graph showing money taken at the Aimhigh Primary tuck shop

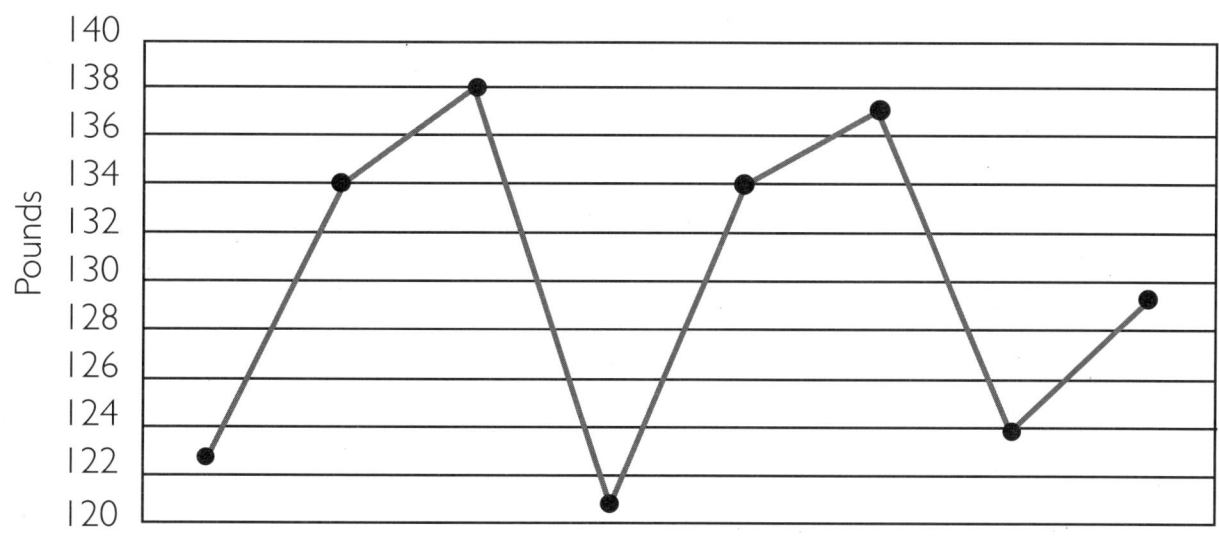

◆ Look at the graph and answer these questions:

1. In which week was £124 taken? _____
2. In which week was £137 taken? _____
3. In which two weeks was the same amount taken? _____
4. Between which two weeks was there the greatest increase in takings? _____
5. Between which two weeks was there the greatest decrease in takings? _____
6. What was the total amount taken over the 8 weeks? _____
7. What was the mean (average) amount taken over the 8 weeks? _____
8. Which weeks were above average? _____
9. Which weeks were below average? _____

◆ Here are some figures from a neighbouring school for the same eight weeks. Use these to plot a similar line graph on the grid above (in a different colour).

◆ Use your graph to make up some questions (on the back of this sheet) for your friends to answer. Remember that you'll need to know the answers!

Figures from Beacon Hill Primary

Week 1	Week 2	Week 3	Week 4	Week 5	Week 6	Week 7	Week 8
£136	£130	£133	£133	£138	£129	£127	£132

HANDLING DATA — RESOURCE BANK

LITTER SURVEY

THE LITTER PROBLEM

GROUP SIZE AND ORGANIZATION
Whole class, then groups of 4 or 5.
DURATION
45 minutes.
LEARNING OBJECTIVES
To identify problems for investigation. To formulate questions about an issue.

YOU WILL NEED
The colour poster; A3 copies of the data handling cycle mini-poster; sugar paper, felt-tipped pens; a flip chart and marker pens (or chalkboard and chalk).

WHAT TO DO
Gather the class on the carpet in front of the colour poster. Ask the children to identify areas of Aimhigh Primary where there is a litter problem. Encourage them to speculate about possible causes; scribe their ideas on the flip chart. Now ask the children to consider how their suggested causes might be investigated. Make suggestions if none are forthcoming: children not using rubbish bins, too many sweets and other packaged snacks being brought to school, badly sited or unused bins and so on.

Break the class into groups of 4 or 5 children. Ask each group to consider what aspect of litter in your school they could investigate. They can use large sheets of sugar paper and felt-tipped pens to 'brainstorm' their ideas. Go round the groups, making suggestions if none are forthcoming. Possible questions for investigation might be:
◆ *In what parts of the school/playground is there a litter problem?*
◆ *What types of litter are found in our school?*
◆ *Are there enough rubbish bins in the school/playground?*
◆ *Are there particular times of the day when litter is a problem?*

Bring the groups together for a general discussion about their ideas. Now ask each group to focus on one question and to discuss among themselves what information they could collect in order to answer it. They will need to think about what kind of evidence they are looking for and when they need to collect it.

Each group should come up with an investigation proposal for you to vet in terms of relevance and practicality. Give each group an A3 copy of the data handling cycle mini-poster, which they can use to track their work on this theme.

ASSESSMENT
Can the children identify suitable questions for investigation? Are their plans feasible?

IDEAS FOR DIFFERENTIATION
Where necessary, help groups to formulate suitable questions.

LOOKING FOR LITTER

GROUP SIZE AND ORGANIZATION
Groups of 4 or 5 (as for previous activity); whole-class discussion; individual writing and drawing.
DURATION
1–2 weeks for surveys; 1 hour for follow-up work.
LEARNING OBJECTIVES
To collect data by undertaking a purposeful enquiry. To represent data using graphs. To draw conclusions from graphs. To record an investigation clearly.

YOU WILL NEED
For survey: gloves; plastic bags; clipboards, paper, pens; a camera (optional). For classroom follow-up: raw data collected by the groups (could be copied and shared or swapped); the glossary mini-poster; squared paper, pencils, rulers.

WHAT TO DO
NB When collecting or sorting litter, the children should always wear disposable gloves and avoid any sharp objects. Some 'litter pickers' (as used by gardeners) would be useful. Check with the school caretaker whether there are any hazard areas that should be avoided, and warn the children of the dangers of picking up litter in streets or parks.

Each group will need a week to collect data. A total period of one to two weeks will allow different groups to monitor and check different areas. The litter survey will need to be integrated with other class activities; the graph interpretation work on this theme (see page 25) could be worked through over the same period. Each group should draw up a survey sheet; if all the group members are using this, they can take turns to do the surveying. Check the children's ongoing surveys regularly. Ask them to consider what types of graphs or charts could sensibly be compiled from their data.

Start the classroom follow-up session with a whole-class discussion, asking each group to describe how they have collected data. Discuss what type of graph

LITTER SURVEY

would be the most suitable to draw. Depending on the children's experience, you may prefer to suggest appropriate types or to have them look at the glossary mini-poster for ideas.

The children should then select some of their information to display graphically. Use the glossary mini-poster to remind them of the different aspects of graph drawing. They could work in their groups, or in pairs, but each child should produce an individual graph. If appropriate, the sets of raw data collected by the groups can be copied and shared; or different groups can work with each other's data. Now ask the children to write down what their graph shows.

Allow further time for the children to discuss their conclusions with the class. Questions to prompt discussion might include: *What times of day are bad for litter? What places in the school are bad? What types of litter are most common? What can be done?* Finally, each group should complete the data handling cycle sheet begun in the previous activity.

An optional (but very worthwhile) follow-up is to collate the children's information and conclusions for a classroom wall display, a poster for the school hall or an assembly presentation. Photographs of litter around the school would enhance displays on this theme. The survey results could even be used to mount a campaign against litter in and around the school, providing further opportunities for monitoring.

ASSESSMENT
How useful is the data the children have collected? Can they construct suitable graphs or charts from their data? Can they draw sensible conclusions?

IDEAS FOR DIFFERENTIATION
Arrange the sharing or exchange of data so as to vary the level of challenge for different groups.

AIMHIGH LITTER PATROL

GROUP SIZE AND ORGANIZATION
Individuals or pairs.
DURATION
45 minutes.
LEARNING OBJECTIVE
To interpret information from bar graphs.

YOU WILL NEED
Photocopiable page 26; squared paper, pencils, rulers; photocopiable page 27, calculators (extension only).

WHAT TO DO
Remind the children of their previous work on surveying litter around the school. Explain that today, they will look at some graphs drawn in Aimhigh Primary to see what information they give. Give each child a copy of photocopiable page 26. Discuss the graph with the children, explaining what it shows. Read through the questions and check that the children understand them. Ask the children to work through the sheet: answering the questions, drawing a graph and using it to answer the final question.

ASSESSMENT
Note how well the children interpret the information. The answers to the questions on page 26 are: **1.** Crisp packets; banana skins. **2.** 15 more. **3.** 27 more. **4.** No more. **5.** Yes. **6.** 92 pieces. **7.** The infants' litter contained much more apple cores and banana skins than the juniors' litter, and much fewer sweet wrappers, crisp packets and pieces of chewing gum. This suggests that the infants' snacks are chosen for them by their parents, and the juniors buy their own snacks.

The answers to the questions on page 27 (see below) are: **1.** 25. **2.** 31. **3.** 23. **4.** More litter is found when the children have just been in the playground (before school, morning break and lunchtime). **5.** The anti-litter campaign caused the rest of the school to be more careful about dropping litter; but over half-term, they forgot about the campaign.

IDEAS FOR DIFFERENTIATION
Older or more able children could go on to work through photocopiable page 27, writing and drawing their answers on the back of the sheet. Some children could enter the data onto a computer database and use the computer to generate graphs.

FURTHER RESEARCH
Older or more able children could research this theme further. For example, they could investigate:
◆ what proportion of litter items are recyclable;
◆ what litter is dropped in the streets near the school;
◆ what litter is dropped in their homes over a weekend.

LITTER SURVEY

Name _____   Date _____

Types of litter

A group of children at Aimhigh Primary analysed the contents of one school rubbish bin from the Junior playground. This graph shows what they found.

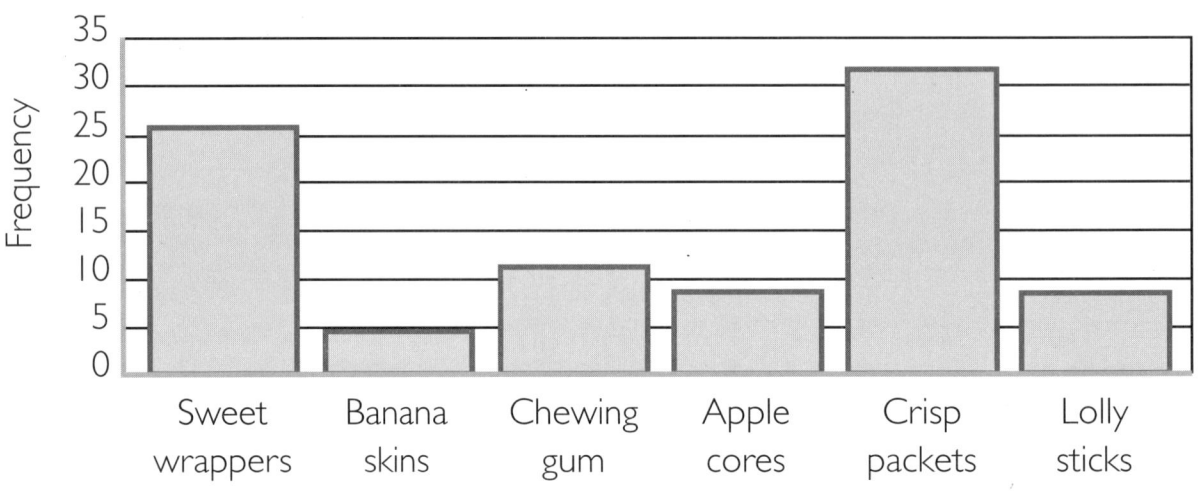

Graph showing the contents of one litter bin at Aimhigh Primary

1. Which was the most common item of litter? _____
The least common? _____
2. How many more sweet wrappers were there than pieces of chewing gum? _____
3. How many more crisp packets than banana skins? _____
4. How many more apple cores than lolly sticks? _____
5. Were there more sweet wrappers than banana skins and apple cores put together? _____
6. What was the total number of pieces of litter collected? _____

7. Another group counted the pieces of litter found in a bin from the Infant playground:
10 sweet wrappers, 17 banana skins, 3 pieces of chewing gum, 22 apple cores, 7 crisp packets, 5 lolly sticks.

◆ Draw a graph to show this information.

◆ What are the main differences between the litter in the Infant playground and the litter in the Junior playground at Aimhigh Primary? What does this suggest about the children?

LITTER SURVEY

Name _____   Date _____

Time and litter

One day, the Aimhigh Primary Litter Patrol counted (and cleared up) the pieces of litter in the main school playground every hour from 9.30am to 3.30pm. This graph shows what they found.

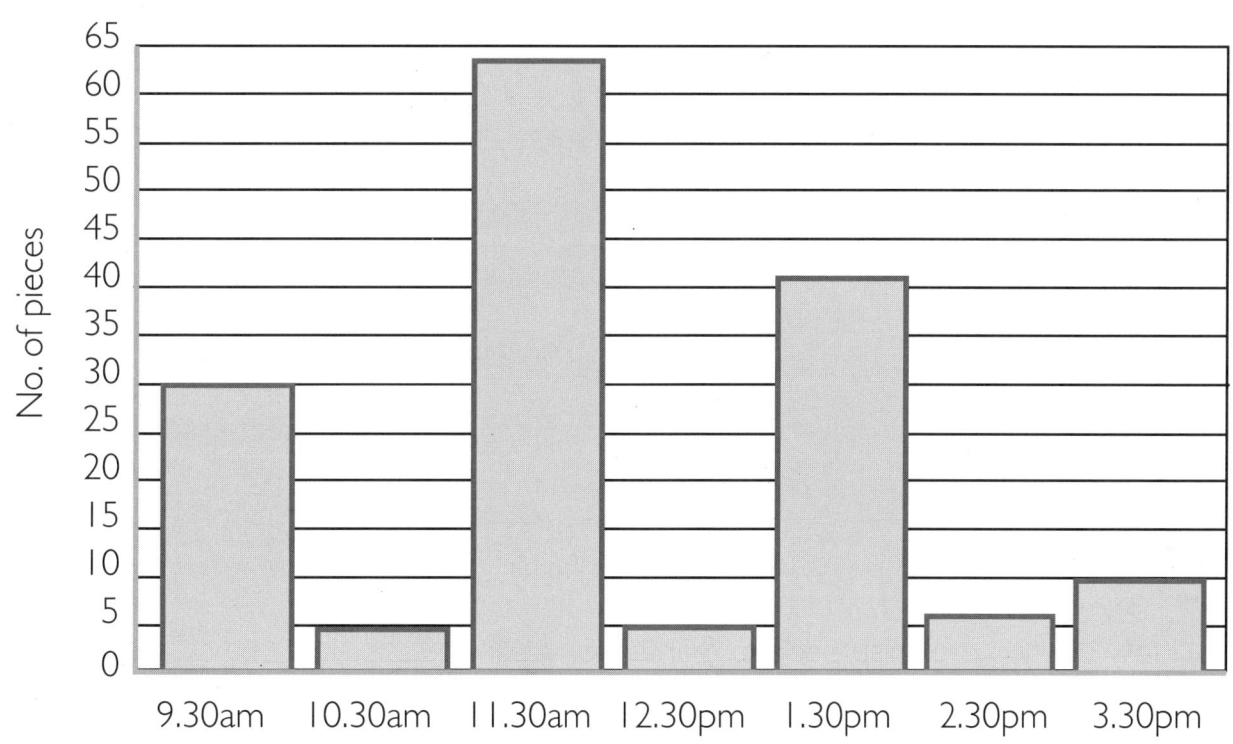

Graph showing the number of pieces of litter found each hour in the playground of Aimhigh Primary

1. How many more pieces were found at 9.30am than at 10.30am?
2. How many more pieces at 1.30pm than at 3.30pm?
3. Calculate the mean (average) number of pieces found each hour.
4. How can you explain the very different quantities of litter found at different times?
5. A fortnight later, after a poster campaign about the litter problem, the Litter Patrol repeated their survey. Two weeks after that (following a half-term break), they repeated it again. This table shows the numbers of pieces of litter they found each hour.
◆ Draw two more graphs to show these results. How can you explain what has happened over this four-week period?

	2 weeks on	4 weeks on
9.30am	15	25
10.30am	2	5
11.30am	8	45
12.30pm	0	12
1.30pm	5	51
2.30pm	5	3
3.30pm	7	10

SPORTS RESULTS

SORT THE SPORTS

GROUP SIZE AND ORGANIZATION
Individuals or pairs.
DURATION
50 minutes.
LEARNING OBJECTIVES
To record information on a table. To interpret the table.

YOU WILL NEED
One set of 'Sports results' cards (see black and white poster) per group; photocopiable page 30; an enlarged (A3) copy of page 30. The 'Sports Results' can be photocopied onto card, cut up and laminated for repeated use; alternatively, a reduced (A4) copy can be given to each child.

WHAT TO DO
Show the 'Sports results' to the children. Ask them: *How can you tell the fastest runner? The longest jumper? The best at skipping? The best at the egg and spoon race?* Note that some of these questions involve looking for the smallest number (times in the 100m and the egg and spoon race), some the largest number (distance in the long jump, number of skips in skipping).

Explain that it will be easier to answer questions about the results if they are tabulated in some way. Give each child a copy of photocopiable page 30, and use an enlarged copy to demonstrate how to fill in one line of the table. The children should then use the 'Sports results' to complete the table before answering the questions on the sheet.

ASSESSMENT
Can the children successfully transfer information to the table? Can they answer the questions on the sheet? Can they make up other questions about the 'Sports results' data? The answers to the questions on page 30 are: **1.** Ayesha; Ben. **2.** Dennis and Evelyn. **3.** No. **4.** Evelyn, Franklin, Georgina, Ingrid and Jason. **5.** Dennis. **6.** 3 people.

IDEAS FOR DIFFERENTIATION
Less able children could work with a more confident partner rather than individually.

EXTENSION WORK
Ask the children to calculate the **range** of the results for each event – that is, the difference between the best and the worst performance.

MEAN, MODE, MEDIAN

GROUP SIZE AND ORGANIZATION
Whole class, then individuals or pairs.
DURATION
50 minutes for each group at the computer.
LEARNING OBJECTIVE
To understand and calculate different kinds of average.

YOU WILL NEED
One set of 'Sports results' cards per group (see previous activity); the completed table from the previous activity; calculators, paper, pens.

WHAT TO DO
Explain the different types of average to the children. The 'Sports results' cards can be used to illustrate this:
◆ **Mean** – take any of the numerical results (such as the long jump results), add up and divide by the number of children (10).
◆ **Mode** – this is the most frequently occurring result. It is only meaningful for discrete data, so use the 'favourite sport' question to illustrate it. Discuss why it makes no sense to look for the mode of the long jump results.
◆ **Median** – this is found by arranging a set of data in numerical order and looking for the middle value. As there are 10 children's results, the median result will be halfway between the results ranked 5th and 6th. The median is useful in cases where an extreme result distorts the mean.

After discussing this, ask the children to find the **mean** and **median** values for the 10 children's height, long jump distance, 100m time, egg and spoon race time and number of skips.

ASSESSMENT
Can the children calculate the mean and median values accurately? Do they understand the differences between these types of average?

SPORTS RESULTS

IDEAS FOR DIFFERENTIATION
Children who find the concept of the median difficult could use the 'Sports results' cards, arranging them in order for each of the events in turn.

More able children could calculate and compare the mean scores of boys and girls in each event. They could also look at the **range** for each event (the gap between the highest and the lowest score).

USING A DATABASE

GROUP SIZE AND ORGANIZATION
Whole class, then pairs.
DURATION
10–15 minutes for demonstration. Two 30-minute sessions for each pair at the computer.
LEARNING OBJECTIVES
To set up a computer database. To use a computer database as a source of useful information.

YOU WILL NEED
A computer with a database program; a floppy disk; photocopiable pages 31 and 32; blank paper, pens.

WHAT TO DO
To prepare for this activity, the 'Sports results' need to be entered onto a computer database. Most modern ones – such as *Junior Pinpoint* (Longman), *Clipboard* or *Information Workshop* (Black Cat Software) – will allow the sorting and graphing processes required by the activity sheet. Alternatively, a spreadsheet program could be used for all the numerical information; this would also allow efficient calculation of averages. Some of the children could be given the task of entering the data, using the instructions on photocopiable page 31; but the main focus of this activity should be on allowing the children to interrogate the database. Use photocopiable page 31 for your own reference if necessary. **NB** When the database has been set up, save it onto a floppy disk as a back-up.

Gather the class around the computer (or do this twice, with half the class each time). Demonstrate some of the basic characteristics of the database. In particular, show the children how to sort records (alphabetically; numerically from highest to lowest or lowest to highest); how to search (for example, for all the children whose favourite sport is cricket); and how to plot different types of graph (in particular, a pie chart and a scattergram).

Give each pair a copy of photocopiable page 32. Organize a roster for the pairs to work at the computer. They should work through some or all of the questions and tasks on page 32, writing on blank paper. Their writing can be attached to any printouts they produce. To help with monitoring, keep a list of the children's names by the computer.

ASSESSMENT
Can the children use the database to sort information? Can they use it to produce graphs of different types? The answers to the questions on page 32 are: **1.** Ayesha; Jason. **2.** Long jump – Georgina; 100 metres – Ayesha; egg and spoon race – Ayesha; skips per minute – Georgina. Smallest to largest – 100m and egg and spoon race (times). Largest to smallest – long jump (distance) and skipping (number of skips). **3.** No real correlation. **5.** Ayesha, Dennis, Franklin, Hassan.

IDEAS FOR DIFFERENTIATION
Children with well-developed computer skills could be paired with those who are less confident. Alternatively, let some of the more able children try the activity first; these children can then be on call to help others who become stuck. (This will free you to continue working with the rest of the class.)

EXTENSION WORK
During a PE or games session, set up some of the sporting activities (or versions of them) that the children from Aimhigh Primary recorded information about. Use this as the basis for your own class database, creating a record of the children's achievements that can be updated regularly. Alternatively, the children can enter the results from their School Sports Day into a database and use it to compare class or house results.

SPORTS RESULTS

Name _____ Date _____

Aimhigh Primary sports results

◆ Use the 10 children's individual records to complete this table:

Name	Height	Favourite sport	Long jump	100m	Egg & spoon	Skips

◆ Now use your table to answer these questions. Use initial letters for the children's names.

1. Who ran 100m the fastest? _____ The slowest? _____
2. Which children did the same number of skips in one minute? _____
3. Did the tallest child jump the furthest? _____
4. Which children jumped a distance greater than their own height? _____
5. Who took more than 1 minute to run the egg and spoon race? _____
6. How many children like tennis best? _____

◆ Check your answers with a friend; then make up some more questions about these results, and write them on the back of the sheet for your friend to answer.

SPORTS RESULTS

Name _____   Date _____

Setting up a computer database

A database record is organized into **fields**, which are the different sections of the data (for example, the various sports events). Each heading or **fieldname** is either **alphanumeric** (words) or **numeric** (numbers).

First, go into the 'Form Designer' and set up a blank form. You will need 7 fieldnames: one for each person's name and six for his or her results. Look at the sports results cards.
- How many of each type of fieldname will you need?

For the 'favourite sports' field, you may be able to set up some **keywords** to save typing in the sport for each person.
- How many different sports have been chosen?

For numeric fields, you should put in the units while designing the form.
- Which fieldnames are measured in metres?
- Which fieldnames are measured in seconds?

When you have designed the form, save it. You are now ready to enter the results for each of the 10 children.

Take turns to fill in the information from the 'Sports results' cards. You should create a new record card for each child. Save your database after each record is completed. Don't worry if you make a mistake – it can always be corrected later.

HANDLING DATA   RESOURCE BANK

SPORTS RESULTS

Name _____   Date _____

Using a computer database

◆ Try some of the following tasks and questions.

1. Sort the records alphabetically (by child's name). Whose record will be first? _____ Whose will be last? _____

2. Sort the records numerically for the long jump, 100 metres, egg and spoon race and skips per minute to see who was best at each.
• Which records should be sorted from the smallest to the largest number?
_____

• Which records should be sorted from the largest to the smallest number?
_____

• Can you explain why? _____
_____

3. Do the tallest people run the fastest? You need to plot a scattergram to find out. Look for a correlation between height and speed.
_____

4. Choose two other numerical categories and find out whether there is any correlation between them.
_____

5. Search for all the children whose favourite sport is football. The computer should now display a set of four records. Whose are they?
_____

6. Use the information about favourite sports to plot a pie chart. What does this chart tell you? _____
_____

7. What else can you find out from the computer database? Write down on the back of this sheet something else that you have found out – and some instructions to help someone else find the same thing.